Unplug Your Family

Recipes for Creative and Meaningful Traditions

Pamela Worth & Tracy Scandlyn

Cover design: Talia Worth
Interior artwork: Lara Levitan

ISBN: 1484064410
ISBN: 978-1484064412

DEDICATIONS

For my incredible husband, Ron, and our four children - Sam, Karly, Talia and Rebecca. Thanks for allowing me to be the crazy mom trying out all my silly and hopefully meaningful ideas with you over and over again. I am so grateful for your openness. I love you all forever and for always. The memory of my father, Seymour Brownstein, with his beautiful, booming voice reading his poetry throughout my childhood has always been one of my greatest inspirations.

Pamela Worth

For my four boys and their amazing dad! Ryan, Jordan, Adam, and Luke, this book is, simply, for you. You are my most favorite people in the whole wide world, my greatest teachers, my deepest joys, my heart and soul. Getting to be your mom is the best blessing of my life! If I lined up all the boys in the world and could only choose four, I'd choose you!!!

Tracy Scandlyn

Contents

INTRODUCTION

As mothers of four children each, we have spent the last twenty years looking for engaging, meaningful, and affordable ways to connect with our sons and daughters. This can be particularly challenging during difficult economic times, but the rewards for doing so are priceless.

One challenge parents of our generation face is that our children are born into a society with a media-driven value system. We are committed to providing traditions for our families that are nature rather than media focused, relational versus "me" focused, and philanthropic instead of consumer focused. Psychologists, authors, and experts in child development feel strongly that traditions and rituals are necessary for the development of healthy families. We agree, and ***Unplug Your Family: Recipes for Creative and Meaningful Traditions*** shows you how to create them even in the midst of financial struggle.

Intentional effort to create relationship-building activities requires thought and planning. Mary Piper, author of *The Shelter of Each Other*, convincingly suggests, "One way to take back our families is through ceremonies and traditions." A sense of identity and a feeling of belonging are promoted by effective traditions. This book's practical, recipe-style format provides easy-to-implement and inexpensive ideas for families.

Co-authors Pamela Worth and Tracy Scandlyn have collaborated to develop these time-tested traditions. You will be given straightforward recipes that will enable you to engage your children in simple yet innovative family experiences which will create lasting memories—and without breaking the bank!

Pamela Worth MA,CLC is the founder of Tiny Treks, a nature exploration program for young children and the founder of "Instructions Included", a subscription parenting solutions service (tinytreks.com). She travels the country giving seminars and lectures. Pam can be reached at www.tinytreks.com.

Tracy Scandlyn is the Executive Director of The Let Them Hear Foundation (letthemhear.org), whose mission is to bring the miracle of hearing to children who are deaf and hard-of-hearing in the United States and around the world.

Okay! Ready for some family fun?

*Cleaning your house
while your kids are still
growing is like shoveling
snow in a snowstorm.*

Phyllis Diller

Making Mundane Moments Count

Sock Mopping

Mopping is never an easy task, especially with hardwood floors throughout the house. We designed "Mopping Mondays" to get our kids involved and have fun while they are at it!

Ingredients:
1 pair damp socks per child
1 room dirty floors (be sure they allow for damp-mopping)

Directions:
1. Place damp socks on child's feet.
2. Allow "ice-skating" throughout room.
3. Throw deliciously dirty socks into laundry basket.

Variation: Place socks on feet AND hands! Be prepared for uncontrollable giggles!

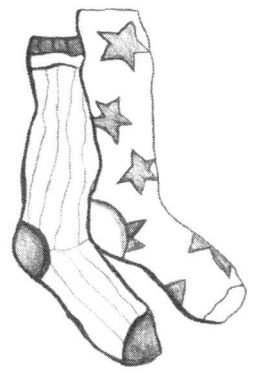

Handy-Wipe Heaven

The person who invented individual cleaning wipes is a genius in our minds! Many a cabinet, door jamb, and countertop has benefitted from this modern convenience. When we are busy with household chores, our little one often want to help by using these delightful dust-busting wipes.

Ingredients:
1 container of handy-wipes–any brand will do.

Directions:
1. Give your child a wipe for each hand.
2. Show them the areas you would like assistance with.
3. Allow child to proceed with the task.
4. Be amazed at how much price they take in their "grown-up" cleaning assignment.
5. Be sure to wash hands after handling the wipes.

Warm Laundry Alert

Having four children means the laundry piles are never-ending! In an effort to enlist help putting the laundry away, we began this tradition as a "call to action."

Ingredients:
Clean, dry, and warm laundry, fresh from the dryer.

Directions:
Begin calling "warm laundry alert" aloud as soon as you remove the clothes from the dryer. Have your children lie down on the couch and simply pile all of the dry clothes on top of them. Allow them to remain under the pile as long as they want, but stay nearby. When they have had enough fun under the heap and begin to leave, you can ask for help folding.

Ten-Minute Tidy

When we notice toys all around the house, we often want to scold, "Clean this up now!" However, we want to make cleaning up fun! We give everyone a ten-minute warning before a ten-minute tidy.

Ingredients:
1 or more child
A basic mess
A stopwatch

Directions:
1. Assign one child the role of time keeper. This person is also expected to participate in the cleaning activity.
2. Set the timer for ten minutes.
3. Allow children to joyfully pick up their mess while an adult supervises.
4. When the timer goes off, all cleaning ceases and hugs are given as rewards.

Sock Party

At the end of the week, our family usually has about ten stray socks sitting on top of the dryer waiting for it's mate. By the end of the month there are twenty-five unclaimed socks looking for their better half. After about six months, an entire basket of unmatched socks looms in the laundry room. Sound familiar??

It is easy to make a game out of rescuing these lonely socks.

Ingredients:
1. Two or more children
2. All mismatched socks (or mittens) needing a partner.
3. A prize (can be as simple as choosing what the family will have for dinner.)
4. A stopwatch

Directions:
1. Gather the children and have them lay on the ground.
2. Toss the socks over the children.
3. Shout "whomever gets the most matches wins!"
4. Begin the stopwatch for the designated amount of time you choose.
5. End with a toss-off by having children toss socks into their sock drawers.

Variation:
Make this a birthday game! We tried and it and the kids had a blast! Their party favor was a new pair of socks!

Prince Ali

Inspiration for activities originate from a variety of influences. For this activity, Prince Ali was invented based on the Disney character that flew the magic carpet in *Aladdin*. What child does not dream of flying through the air?

Ingredients:
Two strong adults.
One child
A study blanket or towel.

Directions:
Place the blanket on the floor and have the child lie on his or her back. Both parents securely grasp the corners of the blanket, lift the child up off of the floor, and swing it gently back and forth while singing a favorite family song. The kids think they are flying, mom and dad get a bicep workout, and the giggles are endless!

Putting Laundry Away

Laundry is an essential component of running a household. After waiting unsuccessfully for the "Magic Laundry Genie" to appear, it is apparent that with a little inventiveness, the little ones will delight in becoming your personal "laundry genie". Putting laundry away can be an entertaining task if presented as such.

Ingredients:
Folded, clean laundry
A child or two.

Directions:
Put the laundry in even piles on the bed - one pile per person. Assign each child a pile to put away neatly. The one who finishes first wins the prize - first dibs on their choice of dip for their apple! (Cheese? Caramel? Peanut Butter?)

Five More Things

Little ones often tire of parent's continual request to "pick up the mess" , and parents grow weary of reminding them. For a quick pick-up trick that will inspire enthusiasm for this mundane chore, give this upbeat activity a shot.

Ingredients:
One upbeat two-minute song
A pair of tiny helping hands
A messy room or two.

Directions:
Play the song at a comfortable, but loud, volume. Challenge the little ones to put away as many items as possible while the song plays. If all items are picked up, they win the prize! They can choose their favorite song and have a special dance with mom or dad in their cleaned up space.

Fun-sized Snickers?
Who's this fun for? Not
me. I need six or seven
of these babies in a row
to start having fun.

Jeff Carlin

Fun With Food

Surprise Shortcake Supper

Sometimes the same old spaghetti, tacos, and meatloaf dinners become uninspired week after week. Shake up your family's expectations with a surprise for dinner - Shortcake Supper! Nothing is more fun at the table then this little treat - especially on a hot summer day.

Let them eat cake!

Ingredients:
One large trifle bowl or other clear serving dish
Fresh strawberries or other fruit
Shortcake (Bisquick works well, but crumbled crackers, pie
    crust, or angel food cake will do.)
Whipped cream
Long spoons for everyone
Festive attitude

Directions:
Prepare the shortcake. Put the shortcake, berries, and whipped cream in the middle of the dining table. Each person uses their long spoons to prepare their own "dinner". Watch with delight as they come to the table to find dessert waiting for them - no green beans in sight!

Taco Tuesday

Feeding our busy families is a daily necessity, whether we have two hours to prepare a gourmet meal, or two seconds to put cream cheese on a bagel. Although we enjoy cooking, caring for active children and managing all of their activities can sometimes squash our chef hats.

Ingredients:

1 pound ground beef, chicken, or turkey
1 package taco seasoning (we prefer Lawry's)
1 can of refried beans or black beans

Taco shells
Grated cheese
Chopped tomatoes
Sour Cream

Lettuce
Onion
Salsa

Directions:

Follow instructions on the seasoning packet to prepare the meat. Place each ingredient in a bowl and arrange them on the table. The kids can assemble their own tacos. It is okay if they do not use every ingredient, but encourage them to try everything, even if it is just on the side.

Easy variation: If you do not have time to cook dinner, there is no harm in succumbing to the occasional "Taco Bell Tuesday." Offer a bowl of apples or grapes to round out the meal.

Easier variation: Eat at Taco Bell to eliminate clean-up.

Easiet variation: Send your spouse to the Taco Bell drive-thru and have the clean-up afterwards!

Martinelli's for a Special Weekly Dinner

Having regular family dinners contributes to a child's feeling of safety and belonging. Choose an easy, simple way to make one dinner per week extra special. We often do just that by adding a sparkling cider, like Martinelli's, to the menu.

Ingredients: Martinelli's, or other brand of sparkling apple juice.

Directions:
Pick a consistent night of the week when everyone will be seated around the table for dinner. Select a different component of the meal each week in which to do something surprisingly different. Examples include serving sparkling apple juice instead of milk, decorating the table as if it were a holiday, bake your own bread, prepare an ethnic dish, or have one of the kids cook for the family. Keep them guessing!

Pancake Sunday

Breaking with tradition and having your spouse prepare Sunday breakfast is a great way for kids to see parents sharing household tasks - and can give you a few extra minutes of shut-eye. And what could be better than pancakes??

Ingredients:
1 happy partner ready for a weekly tradition
Hungry children
Pancake mix
Syrup
Butter

Directions:
Do nothing. It is your spouse's turn!

Upside-Down Dinner

Maybe you did not inherit the "loves to cook" gene. Or maybe you are always on the prowl for creative ways to entertain yourself in the kitchen while providing healthy meals. Why not try serving breakfast at dinner? We are not talking a quick bowl of fruit loops, but a complete meal consisting of fruits, veggies, and protein.

Ingredients:
Eggs
Cheese
Vegetables
Canadian bacon for omelets
Wooden skewers
Fruit for fruit kabobs
Potatoes for hash browns
Juice
Milk.

Directions:
Since the menu is simple, ask your kids to help prepare. They may especially love to make the fruit kabobs! Make it a truly "upside-down meal" by having everyone shower and put on their PJs before they eat.

Hot Cocoa with Grandma

We all know it takes a village to raise a child, and implementing rituals for your child to share with adult friends and family members can enrich the lives of everyone involved. We had an eager grandma who loved a weekly hot cocoa outing with our child. They would have a "tea party" weekly, spending at least an hour in the local cafe sharing hot cocoa, talking, drawing and playing.

Ingredients:
Any eager adult willing to do something on a regular basis with a child.

Directions:
Pick any simple activity for an adult and child to share, and by week two it becomes a ritual. If weekly is not possible, monthly or even yearly works, too!

Rainbows on a Rainy Day

This is a fun and delicious way to teach the colors of the rainbow to little ones, but kids of all ages can help!

Ingredients:
Red, orange, yellow, green, blue, and violet Jell-O
A deep dish (preferably see-through)
A lazy rainy day.

Directions:
Make Jell-O one layer at a time, allowing each layer to gel in between. While waiting, take a walk in the rain, make boats to float in the gutter, or simply enjoy a quiet day inside.

Midnight Ice Cream

It is easy to fall into the rut of being simply "functional," rather than fun, in the lives of our children. Kids typically love surprises, so why not dazzle them with a little midnight goofiness?

Ingredients:
Transportation, a little cash, and a love of surprise.

Directions:
Pretend the evening bedtime routine is proceeding as normal. But... once all the kiddos are tucked in, wait a few minutes before marching right back into their rooms and ordering them up at once! Whisk them away for a late-night ice cream cone, or to the grocery store for ice cream sundae makings. Everyone--parents included-- must keep their PJs on for this extravaganza. The surprise factor, plus parents' willingness to be silly, makes this a frequently-requested treat!

Dinner Co-op

Chances are you are not the only parent on the block looking for ways to reduce dinner-time stress. Try coordinating with one or more families to alternate the cooking of a regular group dinner. This practice not only enriches family life, it strengthens community, and maybe even offers the chance to try dishes you would never make. You may have one very full night of cooking when it is your turn, but remember that many responsibility-free nights will follow!

Ingredients:
Two or more enthusiastic families who live in the same neighborhood.

Directions:
Coordinate a schedule that accommodates all the families nicely. For example, families with two parents who work full-time might choose Sunday nights. If possible, involve families of different ethnicities to enjoy a variety of cuisines. When it is your night off, take pleasure in a late-afternoon trip to the park with your kids. When they ask, "Mommy, can we stay a little longer?" revel in saying yes, knowing that a homemade dinner will be ready by six. (Note: If all else fails on your night, splurge and order in for all the families.)

Awesome Applesauce

When our children were small and apples were too hard for them to chew, we began making homemade applesauce. It is simple, healthy, and kids of all ages can be involved.

Ingredients:
3 pounds apples
1/2 tsp. Cinnamon
1 tsp. nutmeg (optional)
1-1/2 cups water
1/4 to 1/2 tsp. salt
Lemon slices

Directions:
1. Cut the apples into one-inch cubes. Core and peel, or keep the peels on for a healthier sauce.
2. Put all the ingredients into a pot and boil, stirring regularly. (The kids love to stir with a big wooden spoon.)
3. Reduce heat to low and cover the pot.
4. Simmer for about 20 minutes until the apples are soft. May need to add more water.

Now the fun part: Mash the apples with a potato masher. If you do not have one, let the pot cool and put in a sealed bag to smash. It is fun to do this with bare feet.

Additional crafty apple project: Make a large drawing of a tree on butcher paper. Cut an apple in half, and let the children use it to print apples on the tree with paint.

Ethnic Night

Even if you do not live in a diverse community, we all live in a diverse world. With a little research, you may discover wonderful ethnic neighborhoods just outside your door. Celebrating Ethnic Food Night once a month will expose your children to the multi-cultural richness of the world.

Ingredients:
A variety of restaurants in one authentic ethnic neighborhood. If that is not possible, find ethnic restaurants in your neighborhood, or recipes for ethnic meals to be prepared at home.

Directions:

There are many ways to approach Ethnic Night. Do not give up, and remember, this tradition may take practice! Put scraps of paper listing different ethnic foods in a large bowl. Once a month, a different child picks blindly from the bowl. As a group, brainstorm a list of different countries, write them in a notebook, and each month choose from the list. If your child is studying a particular country in school, visit a restaurant that serves that cuisine. Give your child the task of researching the restaurants. For an extra thoughtful experience, write restaurant reviews after the meal, so everyone can give his or her feedback.

Warning: Although Ethnic Night can be exciting, the first visit to a completely different neighborhood may be a push for your kids, especially since they may have never heard of, let alone tasted, many of the foods. Acclimating to such new flavors and surroundings may take a few outings.

Baking Bonanza

Ahhh, baking! The gathering of the family, the gooey dough we all lick off of the spoon, the wonderful smell of freshly-baked cookies. We love doing our baking on Sundays so the kids can have homemade cookies in their lunches all week long (or at least one day). One of our favorite, most fool-proof recipes, Kiss Cookies, makes baking with the family extra simple.

Ingredients:
Flour
Butter
Powdered sugar
Unwrapped chocolate kisses.

Recipe for Kiss Cookies:
2 cups of flour
2 sticks of butter
1-3/4 cups powdered sugar
1 tbsp. vanilla
Unwrapped chocolate kisses
Finely chopped or ground nuts (optional)

Directions:
1. Mix all the ingredients with hands
2. Wrap dough around the kiss. (The dough can be pretty thin around kiss to yield more cookies.)
3. Bake at 350 degrees for eight minutes on an ungreased cookie sheet.

Ritual Sunday Brunch

After a busy week and an errand-filled Saturday, a planned
Sunday outing can be just what the doctor ordered. Whether
you go to church, Sunday school, or just sleep in, squeezing
in two hours for brunch can help end the weekend on a
relaxing note.

Ingredients:
A list of nearby brunch spots.

Directions:
Pick a restaurant and go! We like to let our children do the
deciding. If you stick to it and try a new restaurant every
week, after a year your family will have experienced 52
different restaurants and types of food!

Courage doesn't always roar. Sometimes it is the quiet voice at the end of the day, saying 'I will try again tomorrow.'

Mary Anne Rademacher

What A Difference A Day Makes

Tooth Brushing Song

How many times have you literally pinned down your toddler or preschooler to brush his or her teeth? Watch your power struggles vanish as you institute a tooth brushing song!

Ingredients:
Toothbrush and toothpaste of the child's choosing (this will help empower the child and make him or her more excited to brush)
A song that your child likes and is easy for you to sing (or try our suggestion below).

Directions:
Have the child help put toothpaste on the toothbrush. While brushing or helping to brush, sing this song to the tune of "Rain, Rain, Go Away."

"Germs, germs, go away. We do not want you here today. Up and down, round and round, brush all over (your child's name) tooth town!"

Warning: You may need a longer or shorter song depending on the child's temperament. And remember to keep your fingers out of their mouth; if they want to stop your singing, they may bite!

Pajama Thursday

Today's parents and children are often overscheduled and under-relaxed. We picked Thursday, but Pajama Day can be any day, or even just a chunk of time, where everyone is dedicated to nestling up in their PJs and having no plans. Pajama Thursday is an excellent antidote to our often tightly-wound lives!

Ingredients:
Small children
Pajamas
Scheduled down-time.

Directions:
When everyone wakes up, shout "Pajama Thursday!" This does not mean you can not go outside for a walk; it means not rushing anywhere, not having any plans, and staying in your PJs throughout breakfast, lunch, and maybe even dinner!

Variations:
For some families, setting one day each week is best, but it can also be random. For example, if your kids are school age, four o'clock might be a good time to put on those PJs and chill out.

Disclaimer: You may like Pajama Thursday so much you revaluate your schedule and opt for more pajama days!

High-Low

If your typical family dinner conversation sometimes feels shallow, sparse or even non-existent, this simple game is a great way to deepen the conversation and learn more about each other's lives.

Ingredients:
A table
Listening ears
Open minds.

Directions:
Go around the table and allow each person to share the "high" and "low" of their day. Encourage everyone to really consider what the most positive experience of their day was, and also something that may have not felt quite right. Remind your children to really pay attention, especially when it is not their turn.

Variations:
It may be too much to try this every night, but we recommend picking one night a week when you usually eat together. Or you can play only when company comes over, or only on holidays, or even just once to test it out.

Daddy's Home

(This was written to welcome Daddy home, but the song and arrival can change for whoever walks in the door.)

It is hard to tell who was happier when "Daddy" came home from work when the kids were little – the kids or mom. The kids joy came from fresh energy, and my joy came from another person who had two hands and did not whine. You hear about dads who need down time after a busy day. There was even a book written about giving your husband "cave time" for an hour when he came home from work. Hmmm. We knew that logic was not for us, as the dads would probably be living in a cave today if they really checked out for an hour each night.

We appreciate what great and involved dads our kids do have, and I made up a silly song when our oldest son was a tiny baby. It lightened the mood when daddy came home and, most importantly, it made him feel great. He jumped right into the mix of things the minute he walked in the door. We still sing it often when dad arrives home.

Ingredients:
A song about Daddy coming home. Ours goes like this: "Daddy's home, Daddy's home, Daddy's home. It's the best part of the day. Daddy's home, Daddy's home, Daddy's home, HURRAY! HURRAY! HURRAH! (You can make up your own version).

Directions:
Let the kids sing loudly and jump into Daddy's arms. Mom is often the loudest and *collapses* into his arms!

Bedtime Ritual

Bedtime rituals give beautiful closure to the day, and allow time to bond with your child. Reading stories, giving back rubs, saying prayers, and singing special songs are some of our favorites.

Ingredients:
Parents, children and time.

Directions:
With each of our children, we developed a slightly different ritual.

For our oldest: We read two books. (We were firm on two books because we knew how quickly it could become ten books.) We tucked him in and sang him three songs. "You Are My Sunshine," "I Love You a Bushel and a Peck," and his absolute favorite, "What Did Sammy Do Today?" We made up that song and it went like this: "What did Sammy do today? Do today? Do today? What did Sammy do today? Let's ask mom or dad." When he was an infant it was things like, "Sammy made a big poop today, poop today, and poop today. Sammy made a big poop today. That's what Sammy did." It made it fun for my husband and me, knowing Sammy just liked the singing.

Back Drawings

Everyone loves the feeling of a gentle touch on their backs. Back drawings combine the relaxing effects of massage with the fun of a game. Even teenagers love the gentle touch, and because it is a game, it is acceptable to them.

Ingredients:
Two people and a little imagination.

Directions:
If you children are very young, draw pictures and shapes on their backs and tell them what they are—this is especially welcome during nighttime snuggles. If they are old enough, add letters and play guessing games with the drawings. With older kids you can progress from simple to challenging words. Kids often like to take turns and may ask to draw a picture, shape or word on your back, too.

Warning: Back drawings are relaxing, educational, and feel so good you may extend the bedtime hour.

If you can DREAM it,
you can DO it.

Walt Disney

Once In A Lifetime

Ear-Piercing Ritual

In some cultures, ear-piercing is a ritual that occurs at a young age. In most American families, however, there is no pre-determined age for ear-piercing. We recommend choosing an age that you feel is logical and appropriate for your daughter(s), and upholding the rule despite complaints or begging. Having a set age is especially helpful if you have more than one daughter—the same rule will apply to everyone.

Ingredients:
The conviction that you picked an appropriate age, and the guts to stick to it. Even if you think your daughter(s) may be ready earlier, it is important to uphold your original stance.

Directions:
When the day comes, make it special. Help her purchase a pair of earrings she chooses in advance. Go to a reputable ear-piercing store, and take lots of pictures.

Variations:
Ear-piercing could be tied to another milestone in her life, like a Bat Mitzvah. Or, if you need a great incentive for an ongoing issue, this could be it. You may not set a time, just wait for the appropriate issue for ear piercing to be the incentive.

Recording the First and Last Days of School

If you are like us, you have very few photos of your own school-age years. Now more than ever, technology makes it simple to keep a recorded history of your children's lives.

Ingredients:
A camera, and children who are young enough to not be humiliated by their parents photographing them at school.

Directions:
Get the kids to school a bit early on the first day, arrange them next to the school sign, and snap a picture. They may want to hold up a sign with their name and grade, so you will not forget in a few years (or possibly a few months)! Do the same on the last day, and when you compare it to the first day photo, delight in seeing how much they have grown. The school name is neat to have in the pictures, especially if you move or switch schools.

Warning: Starting by about fourth grade, your children may moan when you ask them to do this. By middle school the humiliation is too much-- unless you can all sneak to school for a picture in the middle of the night!

Bar/Bat Mitzvah Trip

We are lucky enough to have a grandma who asked us what we wanted her to do for our child's Bar/Bat Mitzvah gift. For her oldest grandson in our cousin's family she had purchased a pinball machine. I talked to my sister-in-law and told her my idea of making things more meaningful if, in the future, grandma would take each child on a trip. It could be as simple as an overnight in another city or state, or something more elaborate. The tradition began.

Because we have four children, my mother-in-law decided to double up with two kids and take them on a five-day exploration of London. It was an opportunity they never would have had otherwise, and they got great bonding time with one sibling and their grandma. Because of the pairing, our two middle girls got lucky and were able to go on two trips!

Ingredients:
An eager and loving adult (a special grandma, aunt, friend, etc.) who can afford to travel.

Directions:
Gently share your idea with the generous, loving adult. Explain that it would be more meaningful to mark this transition in a child's life with an experience, rather than a gift.

The Other Mother Party

The invitation came from our close neighbor across the street. Please come to an "Other Mother Party" to celebrate our daughter turning 18 years old. "What is this," I wondered? The card read: "You have all been an important part of our daughter's life, and have helped to raise and parent her. I invite you to find a bead that, to you, represents our daughter, and please join us next Sunday to celebrate her 18th birthday. If you would like to write a paragraph and relate it to the bead, that would be wonderful."

"Wow, I am really in California," I thought. This was so out of the box, but I loved it. This young woman was strong and interesting, and because of this invitation, I ended up writing a long piece about her strength and inner beauty. The party was an afternoon I will never forget, and together a group of "other mothers" made her the most beautiful beaded keepsake necklace with shared words of encouragement and wisdom with her.

Ingredients:
An 18-year-old woman, loving women to surround and celebrate her.

You Are Now a Woman

A girl's first period is a very special yet sensitive time in her life. Taking your daughter out to buy a "You are now a woman" piece of jewelry can be a wonderful, personal way to celebrate this sign of maturity.

Ingredients:
A young woman and her mother, both willing to mark the occasion.

Directions:
It is best to keep the jewelry simple. Many girls are quite embarrassed by the situation and can find overly-exuberant or proud mothers annoying. But there is no harm in assuring your daughter that her first period is a beautiful milestone, and does not have to be a secret.

*Wherever you go, no
matter what the weather,
always bring your own
sunshine.*

Anthony J. D'Angelo

The Seasons of Your Life

Mulch Day

Turning mulching into a party instead of a chore can foster a love of gardening in your children. Being outside in the fresh air, inviting friends to help, and working together to accomplish a task has made this a favorite fall activity for our families.

Ingredients:
Mulch
Small wheelbarrows
Small shovels.

Directions:
Invite all the neighborhood kids over for Mulch Day. Set up a water station, if you are so inclined. Help your worker bees fill their wheelbarrows with mulch to transport. They will feel so grown up, and will love climbing to the top of the pile and squishing their little hands in the warm mulch.

First Day of Summer

The first day of summer begins a period of rest and fun. We have made it a point to begin summer by having no agenda— except for eating popsicles!

Ingredients:
Popsicles (lots of them!) in all flavors.
Directions:
Begin the day by telling your children that it is the first day of summer, and there will be no limit on the number of popsicles they can eat throughout the day. Offer popsicles for breakfast, and watch the smiles spread across their faces. Better yet-- let them catch you eating a popsicle for breakfast too!

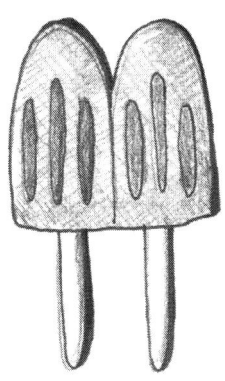

Apple Picking

I used to look forward with incredible joy to my family- of- origin's yearly trip to the apple orchard. I remember my father at the wheel with my mother at his side, and my four older siblings and me piled in the back of the car. Days like this—with all the regular fighting and hassles put aside for a special family outing-- felt so right for me. We even stopped for hot apple cider and caramel apples on the way home. I remember all my friends, who seemed to have much more structured family activities on a daily basis, envied all of our Sunday rituals.

I wanted to adopt this ritual when my own family lived in California, but, despite the amazing fruit produced there, the one fruit the Midwest is better for is apples. This year we were in Chicago in the fall, and on a gorgeous day we all piled in the car for apple picking. It was as wonderful as I remembered. All of our children, ages 3-12, were thrilled to pick their own bag of apples.

With rides and entertainment, the orchard is a bit more upscale now, but we stuck to good old apple picking, and then enjoyed warm apple pie à la mode in the orchard restaurant.

Ingredients:

A vehicle large enough to fit the whole family, and baskets (if they are not provided by the orchard).

Directions:

Even if you have to drive over an hour to visit a family-friendly orchard, it is worth it. Just sit back, relax, and enjoy the car ride.

Disclaimer: Times have changed, because my kids looked at me like I was insane when I suggested they bring an apple to their teacher the next day.

Homemade Doughnut Day

Nothing tastes better on the first cool fall day than homemade doughnuts. This tradition is so popular that even the neighborhood children will begin to ask when it is Doughnut Day!

Ingredients:
Refrigerator biscuits from your local supermarket, powdered sugar, and frying oil.

Directions:
Heat the oil in a large skillet. While the oil is heating, punch holes in the individual roll dough pieces. Fry the pieces until golden brown. Stir together powdered sugar and a small amount of milk until you have a glaze consistency. Drizzle glaze over the hot doughnuts and serve. The doughnuts will be eaten as fast as you can fry them!

The Magic Pumpkin

Though we are the first to admit we love Halloween and all its sweet treats, the sheer excess of trick-or-treat candy our kids sometimes bring home can be overwhelming. The Magic Pumpkin helps alleviate the potential sugar overload while allowing the kids to enjoy the holiday.

Ingredients:
Paper
Pencil
A small gift of your child's choice
Halloween candy.

Dear Magic Pumpkin,

Here is all of my candy besides the 28 pieces that I kept. Rebecca and I have chosen to join our candy together in return for one big present. We would greatly appreciate a dippin' dots maker. It can be found at toys r us. Thank you so much!

Love, Talia

Directions:

The night before Halloween, ask your kids to dictate or write a few choices of what gift they would like from the Magic Pumpkin, a special pumpkin that visits people's homes on Halloween night. Instruct your children that if they leave out all their candy, the Magic Pumpkin will trade it for a present. (This may be extra exciting for Jewish children who never experience Santa Claus.)

Warning: Remember, it is only candy they are giving up, not their entire toy closet. Keep the presents simple. And of course, this may not work for all children. One of our children would not even consider trading her coveted candy for a silly toy-- but it was worth a try!

Pumpkin Carving

Everyone loves the pumpkin patch! Together with our families, we drive to a local patch one week before Halloween. Each child picks out a pumpkin that he or she can carry by themselves to the car. (This works well when they are small, but becomes more expensive when the teenagers pick larger and larger specimens!) Consider ordering dinner in on carving night to allow plenty of time for all of the design phases.

Ingredients:
Pumpkins
Carving knife
Scoopers
Paper towels
Drawing supplies
A colander.

Directions:
Each child first draws a picture of what they imagine their Jack-O-Lantern will look like. Next, help the little ones with the initial carving.

Variations:
Host a pumpkin-carving party and invite the neighborhood. If you have just moved, this is a great way to get to know your neighbors.

Warning: This is a huge mess if you truly let the kids create, but it is worth it!

Family Flag

Family traditions will long be remembered by your children, and one of the most creative activities you can do together is to design a family crest or flag.

Ingredients:
Butcher paper or fabric (if you are ambitious)
Art supplies.

Directions:
Explain that a family crest or flag represents the family's values and/or favorite activities. Divide the area of your flag into one section per family member. Each person has the pleasure of designing his or her own area. Parents should allow for creativity and age-appropriate artwork. Remember, the object is not to complete a Windsor-worthy masterpiece. Rather, you are collaborating on a treasure the whole family will enjoy for years.

Variation:
If your family enjoys this activity, design a new flag or crest each year. Your interests and activities will change as your children grow.

Winter Picnic

Cold weather, rain and snow can make the winter last forever. A winter picnic is a fun, easy way to alleviate the doldrums while staying warm inside!

Ingredients:
A big blanket
An indoor space large enough for the whole family to sit on the floor
Cute picnic baskets for your food.

Directions:
Arrange the blanket and picnic baskets in the middle of your family room or basement. When you call everyone down for dinner, shout, "It is a winter picnic!" Eating on a blanket in the middle of winter adds a really fun, surprising element to the night.

Warning: Keep the food easy to clean-- no marinara sauce or goopy foods.

My father gave me the greatest gift anyone could give another person, he believed in me.

Jim Valvano

So Glad You Were Born

Birthday Wake-up

Parents have been playing music for children since research showed the benefits of using a music on a pregnant belly, to stimulate the unborn child with classical music. My husband and I are more of the rock 'n' roll types, so we started a birthday wake-up tradition the year our oldest son, Sam, turned one. Sam called us from his crib and we both eagerly woke up, ready to greet our crawling one year old.

We went into the living room and blasted The Beatles' "Birthday" song off the *White Album*. We twirled and danced around the living room with Sam overjoyed and giggling through it all. We bought Sam his own CD of the *White Album* when he was five. It has become a family tradition for everyone's birthdays. Often it is the alarm that wakes us up on our special day. We often have to drag our adolescent Sam off the couch to participate in the ritual for his younger sisters, but we seem to still be able to get a smile on his face while we sing.

Ingredients:
CD of The Beatles' *White Album* (It comes in a two CD pack, or download). The song is called "Birthday."

Directions:
Play the music and crank up the volume. Hold your child close, twirl plenty and laugh often.

Special Plate

As you might have guessed, celebrating is huge in our households. While we have been known to create parties for just about everything, birthdays are an occasion to go all out. Try ringing in your next family birthday with a special family plate.

Ingredients:
Choose a plate that stands out from the rest, is unusual in its design or color, and/or has some significance to the family.

Directions:
Beginning with breakfast, use this special plate to serve the birthday boy or girl every meal of the day. Decorate their place setting in a way that is unique to that child.

Draw the Birthday Boy/Girl

This is a fun way to have a life-size memento of your child on his or her birthday.

Ingredients:
Colored markers
A roll of craft paper
Plenty of family and friends.

Directions:
Have the birthday child lie on the floor atop the craft paper. Trace around the child's shape with a dark marker. After he or she gets up, have all family and friends present fill in the outline, portraying the birthday child's clothes, physical features, hair color, and anything else they can think of. Encourage everyone to express his or her artistic flair! When finished, carefully roll up the paper and store—you will want to compare if you do it again next year!

Breakfast in Bed

In our homes, it is imperative that the birthday person sleeps in and receives a gourmet breakfast in bed– especially if that person is mom!

Ingredients:
Food of the birthday person's choice.

Directions:
Allow the kids to prepare, or help prepare, breakfast for the adult. When it is a child's birthday, involve the entire family in the process.

Warning: When the kids are little and you are trying to let mommy or daddy sleep in on their special day, it is tough to contain the excitement. When the kids are teens, it is hard to wait all day to wake them for breakfast!

Choose Your Birthday Meal

In this straightforward and popular tradition, the birthday person gets to choose the site of their special birthday dinner. Depending on finances, it can be a favorite homemade dinner or a favorite restaurant.

Warning: You may end up spending several birthdays in a row at your local Taco Bell. Thank goodness mom and dad can choose their favorites, too!

Let's Give Something Back

If you are reading this book, you probably have healthy food for every meal and more than enough toys, clothes and gadgets. This tradition will help your child learn that much of the joy of receiving is the joy of giving back.

Ingredients:
A grateful family, and presents.

Directions:
Once they receive all of their birthday presents and before they use them, encourage your children to choose an equal number of toys or clothes they already own to donate to charity.

Variation:
Ask your child to donate just one of their gifts, especially if it is a duplicate. Some especially large-hearted children may consider asking for donations to a cause of their choice rather than receiving a gift of their own.

Warning: It is much harder for the little ones to part with their toys, even if they have not looked at it in a year.

Circle of Encouragement

The saying goes that five encouragements are needed to balance every one criticism. There is no place like home for receiving words of appreciation and gratitude.

Ingredients:
Fifteen minutes and enough chairs for everyone.

Directions:
Select one family member to be the recipient of the gift of encouragement. Arrange a circle of chairs around the chosen person's seat. Take turns expressing thoughtful words about him or her.

Sing-Along Night

Is there a child or parent in your family who plays an instrument seriously, or even just dabbles? If so, a regular sing-along not only nurtures family togetherness, it gives your musician a chance to squeeze in a little extra practice!

Ingredients:
A musical instrument, a person who can (even somewhat) play a musical instrument, and a good music book with songs the kids know.

Directions:
Pick a night of the week that will mostly work in your house, gather the family 'round, and sing!

Variations:
If no one can play an instrument, just sing.

Warnings: Older kids can be much less enthusiastic (to put it nicely) than little ones. If this is the case with your family, remind them in advance that it is Sing-Along Night, and ask them to be pleasant.

How wonderful it is that no one need wait a single moment to start to improve the world.

Anne Frank

Do Unto Others

Garage Sale

Encourage your kids to have a charitable garage sale. It can motivate you to clean up, organize and eliminate old or unused stuff while simultaneously helping others. With a little goal-setting, your kids may beg to have a garage sale every year!

Ingredients:
Gently used clothes and toys.

Directions:
Set a goal to make enough money to purchase something someone else needs, or to make a significant donation to the charity of your choice. Choose a date and begin cleaning up a few weekends beforehand—this is a chance for the whole family to help each other.

Allow the kids to implement the plan from start to finish by creating signs, posters, banners, and flyers for the neighborhood. Price all items and work with the kids during the garage sale.

Carnival for a Cure

If your child or your child's friend or classmate has a serious medical condition, hosting a carnival to raise funds to support the cause can be fun and meaningful.

One of our oldest daughter's best friends had juvenile diabetes. Karly was in a big group of friends and she was the only one celebrating a Bat Mitzvah. We decided to create a Carnival to raise money for Juvenile Diabetes Research Foundation (JDRF) as her mitzvah project, which was mandatory in our family. We involved all nine of Karly's group to advertise, create and run the carnival. We raised over $1000 the first year. It has now become a tradition, and our youngest daughter, Rebecca, now has a good friend with juvenile diabetes. We included every girl in her grade who wanted to participate and at last count we have 39 girls who will be involved in this year's carnival. I am retiring from running it and our 16 year old daughter, Talia, has completely taken over the communications, meetings, etc.

Ingredients:
A cause you believe in
Eager children up for a challenge
Advertising flyers
A physical location.

Neighborhood Walk-a-thon

Each spring, our neighborhood council chooses a family in need of support due to illness, the birth of a baby, death of a loved one, aging, or other trying circumstances. As a group, we brainstorm ways to assist creatively. One year we raised money for an elderly neighbor's yard service by hosting a neighborhood walk-a-thon.

Ingredients:
A neighborhood council or otherwise motivated group of neighbors, a family or individual in need, and creativity.

Directions:
Begin this thoughtful tradition by suggesting it at your next neighborhood council meeting. You may need to volunteer as chairperson of the event for the first year. After that, there will be others vying to lead as this becomes a neighborhood favorite.

Variations:
Your group can host bake sales, walk- or dance-a-thons or babysitting co-ops – your creativity is your only limit.

Closet Cleaning

If philanthropic events and socials are common in your town, chances are your neighbors' closets are full of fancy ball gowns, cocktail dresses and holiday attire. Typically, these frocks are worn to one or two events, and then end up crowding the closets. Instead of taking up space in the dark ends of your wardrobe, why not put those garments to good use and host a closet cleaning for charity? One example is donating party dresses for high school students during prom and homecoming seasons.

Ingredients:
Unused party attire, and a willingness to part with all that velvet and lace.

Directions:
Invite your friends and neighbors to gather and drop off their dress-up clothes to you on a specific date. Contact your local high school and arrange an evening of "free shopping" for the students. Gather your friends, and enjoy one of the best shopping experiences of your lifetime. Local stores may provide mannequins, hanging garment racks, and other store accessories you may need.

MS Walk

My sister-in-law has multiple sclerosis (MS). Modern research and incredible drugs have helped her stay healthy for the past ten years--but she is one of the lucky people. Every year we walk in the MS walk with her team, WORTH THE WALK. At first she was hesitant to ask friends and family to share this morning with her. But she overcame her fear, and since has done an amazing job writing a beautiful letter and organizing a fun group to walk every year. This has become a ten year family tradition, and even the teenagers do not complain about getting up early. We have even had a child or two in a cast doing the walk, limping along.

Directions:
Find a cause or share someone else's, and make a yearly ritual around a bike ride, a walk, a run, a bowl-a-thon or a skate-a-thon. It is something the kids remember, and you are supporting a special person in your life.

Warning: Walks like these are typically held very early in the morning.

Change for Change

Maintaining a "Change for Change" jar in a centralized area of your home is a quick, easily-accessible way to raise money for donating. You may consider donating to various causes that come up at school, places of worship, or in your neighborhood. Regularly collecting for and donating to charity contributes to community-building, and fosters a sense of philanthropy in your children.

Directions:
Break out the stickers, markers, ribbons, scraps of wrapping paper and tape, and have the family decorate a jar together. Consider getting others involved by hosting a Change for Change jar-decorating party, so that other families and friends can share in the tradition.

Warning: When in a rush, you may be tempted to dip into the jar for lunch money!

Soup Kitchen

We received a letter from our temple asking if anyone wanted to prepare and serve a dinner at the Inspiration Cafe soup kitchen in Chicago. Our family signed up for a date that would take place a few months later. Our responsibility was to shop, cook (in the cafe kitchen), and be waiters and waitresses to serve individuals and families a lovely meal. This was a family experience that was made even more special as our son was home from college for spring break. Together we shopped, cooked, and served food to about 80 deserving and lovely people. We were inspired knowing that individuals who may be struggling to get on their feet are likely to improve their mental/emotional health when they share a meals together. This simple gesture can then positively transform their aspirations in life.

A sweaty four hours later, we sat together not just as a family, but as a team, who had come together with other volunteers to enjoy the meal we had prepared. The satisfaction of serving others and an appreciation of people from all walks of life established a sense of compassion that they will carry with them throughout their lives.

Ingredients:
A sense of compassion.

Directions:
There are many opportunities for families to have first hand experiences helping others.

Warning: One of our kids said after our first visit, "Can we do this every Sunday?"

Beach Clean-up

Earth Week or the first day of spring are perfect times to take the family to the beach for a post-winter clean-up.

Ingredients:
Gloves
Garbage bags.

Directions:
Try setting a goal, like picking up enough cans to fill an entire garbage bag. You can go as a family, or join an organized clean-up group.

Earth Week

Be it Earth Day, Earth Week, Earth Month, or any time of year, try committing to one regular, family-oriented, eco-conscious activity. It could be as simple as walking to the store once a week instead of driving.

Warning: Follow-through can be hard, so choose goals that are realistic and achievable.

Here are more ideas:

One day a week, prepare a completely waste-free lunch.
Pick one park per week in which you and the kids pick up trash for ten minutes, and then play for ten minutes.
Buy no prepackaged, individual-serving-sized foods for a month.
Send everything for lunch in recyclable packaging.
Have a party with more than ten guests and do not use paper plates. (You will be shocked by how easily your friends will bond while washing dishes together.)
Encourage your kids to pick up five pieces of garbage a day as they walk to school or walk the dog.

On the first day of spring, go to a local beach or lake and pick up trash.

Reuse items like toilet paper rolls and egg cartons for craft projects.

For more ideas go, visit the *For What It's Worth* blog at tinytreks.blogspot.com.

Unplug
Your Family
Recipes for Creative and Meaningful Traditions

We hope you enjoy the ideas. There is nothing sweeter than holding your child close and laughing together. The focus on family fun, creating new traditions and cutting down on media and TV time brings its own rewards.

It is so important for all of humankind to stay connected with nature. Through wonderful hikes, music, crafts, snacks and stories, **Tiny Treks** families enjoy the natural world while staying connected to each other in the process. For information on programs with children, get in touch with Tiny Treks. Visit tinytreks.com and the *For What It's Worth* blog at tinytreks.blogspot.com.

A portion of the proceeds from **Tiny Treks** books goes to charitable causes that benefit the needs of children.

Made in the USA
San Bernardino, CA
07 March 2015